The Iroquois
and Their History

REVIEW COPY
COURTESY OF
COMPASS POINT BOOKS

by Genevieve St. Lawrence

Content Adviser: Bruce Bernstein, Ph.D.,
Assistant Director for Cultural Resources
National Museum of the American Indian, Smithsonian Institution

Reading Adviser: Rosemary G. Palmer, Ph.D.,
Department of Literacy, College of Education,
Boise State University

COMPASS POINT BOOKS
MINNEAPOLIS, MINNESOTA

Compass Point Books
3109 West 50th Street, #115
Minneapolis, MN 55410

Visit Compass Point Books on the Internet at *www.compasspointbooks.com*
or e-mail your request to *custserv@compasspointbooks.com*

On the cover: While a papoose naps on its board, Iroquois women grind corn or dried berries,
French engraving, 1664

Photographs ©: The Granger Collection, New York, cover, 8, 14, 17, 28, 32; Prints Old & Rare,
back cover (far left); Library of Congress, back cover, 33; North Wind Picture Archives, 4, 16, 18,
20, 30; MPI/Getty Images, 5, 6, 27, 31; Svetlana Zhurkin, 7; David Muench/Corbis, 10; Carnegie
Museum of Natural History, 12; Mary Evans Picture Library, 15, 24, 34; Reco International, 19;
Photodisc, 21; Smithsonian American Art Museum, Washington, D.C./Art Resource, N.Y., 23;
Gay Miller, 25; Stock Montage, 26; Canadian Heritage Gallery ID #10058, National Archives of
Canada #C-1959, 35; AP Photo/Kevin Rivoli, 36; Bettmann/Corbis, 38, 40; Kit Breen, 39.

Editor: Julie Gassman
Designer/Page Production: Bradfordesign, Inc./Bobbie Nuytten
Photo Researcher: Svetlana Zhurkin
Cartographer: XNR Productions, Inc.
Educational Consultant: Diane Smolinski
Library Consultant: Kathleen Baxter

Managing Editor: Catherine Neitge
Creative Director: Keith Griffin
Editorial Director: Carol Jones

Library of Congress Cataloging-in-Publication Data
St. Lawrence, Genevieve.
  The Iroquois and their history / By Genevieve St. Lawrence.
      p. cm.—(We the people)
  Includes bibliographical references and index.
   ISBN 0-7565-1272-7 (hardcover)
1. Iroquois Indians—History—Juvenile literature. 2. Iroquois Indians—Social life and
customs—Juvenile literature. I. Title. II. We the people (Series) (Compass Point Books)
   E99.I7S79 2006
   974.7004'9755-dc22   2005003676

TABLE OF CONTENTS

THE GREAT LAW OF PEACE

A long time ago, before Europeans came to North America, the Iroquois nations lived in conflict with one another. The Mohawk, Oneida, Onondaga, Cayuga, and Seneca nations did not trust each other. When a Mohawk warrior killed an Onondaga man, an Onondaga killed a Mohawk in return. With every death, the war continued.

In the middle of the wars, a Huron Indian man named Deganawida came to the Iroquois to share visions he had for them. Deganawida, who was called the Peacemaker, wanted the people to stop killing each other,

4

The Iroquois nations fought many bloody battles with each other.

work together, and form a new government. He traveled among the Iroquois, sharing his message of peace.

One of the people the Peacemaker met in his travels was Hiawatha, an Onondaga chief. Hiawatha's wife and all three of his daughters had died. Hiawatha had gone into the woods to grieve for his family. There, Hiawatha met the Peacemaker. The Peacemaker gave Hiawatha some beautiful shell beads and told him to leave the woods and come with him.

It is said that the Peacemaker had a stutter, so Hiawatha became the spokesperson for the peace plan.

Hiawatha accepted the shell beads and joined the Peacemaker on his journey. They traveled to the five Iroquois nations. When the chiefs heard the Peacemaker's words, they accepted his plan, known as the "Great Law of Peace."

Only one chief, Atotarho of the Onondaga nation, did not accept the plan. Atotarho was an evil man, with snakes crawling in his hair. His twisted body and clawlike

6

Atotarho tied snakes in his hair to scare others.

hands frightened everyone. He did not listen to the Peacemaker, and he refused the new peaceful laws.

The chiefs who had accepted the Peacemaker's plan decided to go to Atotarho with Hiawatha and the Peacemaker. They found Atotarho deep in a swamp. This time, all the chiefs sang a powerful song to Atotarho. When he heard their song's peaceful words, his eyes and ears opened. Hiawatha came to him and combed the snakes from his hair. The chiefs massaged Atotarho's crooked body, and soon it straightened. Hiawatha told Atotarho that the Onondaga nation would be the keepers of the council fire for the great confederacy of the Iroquois. Then Hiawatha recorded the Great Law of Peace by creating a patterned belt of colored beads called a wampum.

An artist's interpretation of the Hiawatha belt shows the five symbols which represent the five Iroquois nations.

7

The Peacemaker described the new law as an imaginary house that stretched over all five Iroquois nations, uniting their people. The law brought peace and created the Iroquois Confederacy. To this day, the members of the Iroquois Confederacy come together. They remember the good words of the Peacemaker and Hiawatha, and the Onondaga nation still keeps the council fire.

8

Chiefs from the five nations gather around the Peacemaker in a French engraving from the early 1700s.

WHO ARE THE IROQUOIS?

The Iroquois have lived in the woodlands of the northeastern United States and southeastern Canada for at least 1,000 years. No one is sure where they migrated from, but some historians believe they moved there from what is now the southern United States.

In the woodlands where they settled and built villages, there were thick forests, wild plants, and plenty of deer, beaver, and bear to hunt. The men hunted and fished from the Hudson River in New York to the Great Lakes.

Around 500 years ago, the tribes of the five Iroquois nations often fought over hunting grounds and good land for crops. When the Peacemaker's law created the Iroquois Confederacy, the wars between the tribes ended. Although the exact date is unknown, historians believe the alliance was created by 1600. In about 1722, the Tuscarora Indians joined the Confederacy after moving to the area from North Carolina.

Area Indian tribes called the Hudson River "Muhheakunnuk" or "river that flows two ways." The flow occasionally changes direction during the Atlantic Ocean's high tide.

The Iroquois received their name from Algonquian tribes, who called them "snakes" or "enemies." When the French fur traders heard the Algonquian word, they wrote it down as "Iroquois." The Iroquois call themselves the Haudenosaunee, or "People of the Longhouse." The Iroquois Confederacy is also called the Iroquois League or the Six Nations.

Today, about 45,000 Iroquois live in New York, Wisconsin, and Oklahoma. Another 21,000 live on reserves

in Ontario and Quebec provinces in Canada. Some
Iroquois live on reservations, but many more live in cities
all over the United States and Canada.

Iroquois reservations are located in the United States and Canada.

THE THREE SISTERS

The Iroquois raised more than half their own food, hunting and gathering the rest. Their main crops were corn, beans, and squash, or the "three sisters" as the Iroquois called them. As Chief Louis Farmer said, "We plant them together, three kinds of seeds in one hole.

The three sisters are a common theme in Iroquois sculptures.

They want to be together with each other, just as we Indians want to be together with each other. So long as the three sisters are with us we know we will never starve."

Iroquois land was covered with forests, streams, and lakes. The tribes built villages near water and planted their crops nearby. The men cut down trees to clear land for planting. The women then planted their three crops together. After 10 or 20 years, many villages had to move to a new location. Planting the same crops every year wore out the soil.

Women stayed near the village year-round. In the spring, they tapped maple trees and boiled the sap into syrup to sweeten many foods. Before the crops ripened, the women and girls collected wild plants and vegetables. In the summer, they picked strawberries, blackberries, and raspberries. They dried the berries in the sun and saved them for winter.

The men spent long periods of time away from the village. They sometimes left for a month or more to hunt or fish. They hunted deer, beavers, rabbits, and birds. The animals provided meat, hides for clothing, and bones for tools and sewing needles. The Iroquois also hunted black bears. They used the bear hide for blankets and ate the meat. The Iroquois smeared bear fat on their skin for protection against insects.

A French illustration from 1664 shows Iroquois women grinding corn while a baby naps.

The lakes and streams were full of many kinds of fish. The men fished with spears or nets to catch salmon, bass, trout, and perch. In the winter, they caught fish through a hole in the ice. Some fish was eaten fresh. The rest was dried or smoked and saved for later.

The Iroquois land was home to the best soil and hunting grounds in the northeastern United States. The good land provided enough food for many families. Some large villages supported 3,000

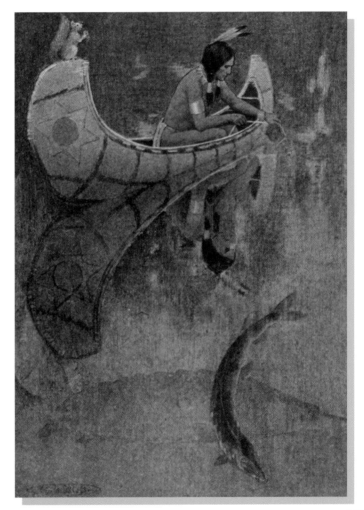

The Iroquois men often fished from a canoe.

15

people. As Chief Canasatego said in the 1700s, "We had then room enough, and plenty of deer, which was easily caught."

Deer hunting parties left the village after harvest and returned in midwinter.

PEOPLE OF THE LONGHOUSE

The Iroquois built their villages on hills with steep slopes. After they cleared land for their homes, they built a tall pole fence called a palisade. The men built steps and platforms on the back of the palisade. They climbed to the platforms to keep a lookout for enemies. The hills gave them a good view of the surrounding land.

Palisades also protected the village from blowing snow in the winter.

17

Groups of related people lived together in one house. These groups were called clans. All the members of a clan were related through the oldest woman in the group, who was called the clan mother. Each clan had a name taken from nature, such as bear, turtle, wolf, or deer.

The traditional Iroquois home was called a longhouse. Although many families shared the longhouse, each had a separate space along the walls.

To build a longhouse, the men first made pole frames from young trees they cut down. Women stripped elm bark and flattened it into shingles. They covered the frames with these shingles and used more poles to hold them in place. A path ran down the center of each house. Every 20 feet (7 meters), two families shared a fire pit. Holes in the ceiling above the fires let smoke escape.

Symbols of Iroquois clans

Longhouses were often 200 feet (61 meters) long. They had a door opening at each end.

Clan members worked together in their fields and shared their harvest in the fall. The women also worked together indoors. They prepared food, wove baskets, and sewed clothing. Young girls and boys helped their mothers plant crops, cook meals, and sew.

Men helped to clear fields and build the longhouses. When they weren't away hunting or trading, they made bows, arrows, and animal traps. They also carved tools such as hoes and scrapers for removing the hair from animal skins. When boys were eight or nine, their fathers and uncles taught them how to hunt and fish.

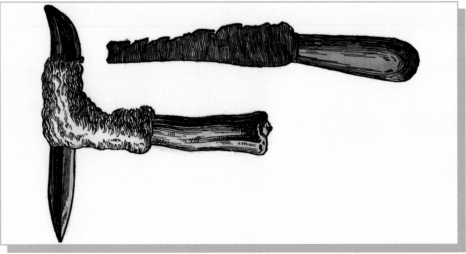

Iroquois men made weapons, such as knives and tomahawks.

CELEBRATE AND GIVE THANKS

The Iroquois year had 13 moons. The people celebrated each moon with a special ceremony. For example, the Midwinter Ceremony was held in January or February when the midwinter new moon appeared. This ceremony lasted for many days. To start the ceremony, men wearing masks ran through each longhouse. They stirred the ashes in the fire and invited the others to join in the festivities.

The Midwinter Ceremony included

The Iroquois gave each of the year's 13 moons a different name.

dancing, feasts, and games. It also included dream guessing. The Iroquois believed dreams held important messages for the dreamer. The messages could even be cures for illnesses. Dreamers came to each longhouse and shared their dreams with the people there. The people would guess what these dreams meant. They gave the dreamers objects or ideas to help them understand the message of their dreams.

Each moon's ceremonies were different, but they all gave the clans a chance to come together. During celebrations in the summer and winter, each clan mother gave names to the clan's new babies. When clan members died, their names went back to the clan mother. She chose when to give these names to new babies. This way, no two living people in the clan had the same name.

The celebrations were also a good time for mothers to look for marriage partners for their sons and daughters. Young people had to marry outside their

A 1830s painting by George Catlin shows an Iroquois woman and her baby in a cradleboard.

clan. The older women of the longhouse had to approve the marriage. After a wedding, the family exchanged gifts, and the new couple went to live in the bride's longhouse.

A French illustration of a traditional Iroquois marriage ceremony

Their children became members of the mother's clan.

After the ceremonies, many people played games. The bowl game was played with six peach pits in a wood bowl. One side of each pit was painted black. Players took turns thumping the bowl on the ground. If at least five pits turned up the same color, the player collected a point.

The Iroquois gave thanks at the beginning and end of every ceremony they held. They believed the world is made up of sacred spirits. The plants, animals, water, earth, and sky all have spirits. The Iroquois thanked the spirits with a thanksgiving speech, which is still used today.

The speech varies from nation to nation. Some speeches begin by thanking the people. "Today we have

Clan symbols were painted on the bowl used in the bowl game.

gathered and we see that the cycles of life continue. We
have been given the duty to live in balance and harmony
with each other and all living things. So now, we bring
our minds together as one as we give greetings and
thanks to each other as People."

The speech continues by thanking the earth
mother, the winds, and the Creator. The Iroquois believe
that the balance of nature depends on thanking nature
for what it provides.

Iroquois festivals often included dancing to drums and shaking rattles.

THE AX MAKERS COME

In the early 1500s, French traders explored the St. Lawrence River in Canada. At first, there were only a few traders. Later, the French built forts and towns along the St. Lawrence. In the early 1600s, Dutch traders sailed up the Hudson River in New York. They built Fort Orange, near Albany on the Hudson River. The Europeans traded

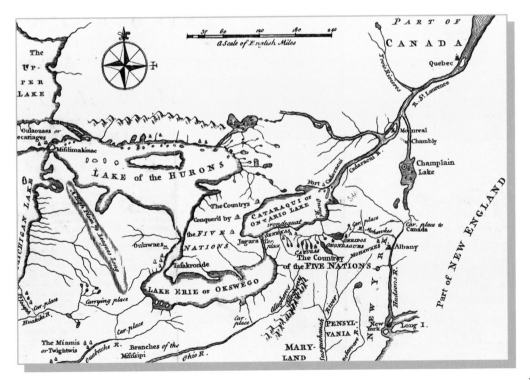

A map of Iroquois land in 1723

27

items like tools, beads, and pots in exchange for animal furs. They wanted beaver fur, which was used to make hats in Europe.

At first, the Iroquois were happy to trade with the Europeans. They wanted the traders' guns and knives. But the settlers also brought diseases. In 1634, measles and smallpox infected the Iroquois. Everyone in the villages became sick, and more than half died.

Although the Iroquois wanted guns and knives, they often received tools and glass beads in return for their furs.

By the late 1600s, the Europeans began to fight with each other over the fur trade. Some Indian tribes chose to fight in the fur wars and joined sides. Before deciding whether or not to join a side themselves, the Iroquois Confederacy called a meeting.

Each nation sent chiefs to the council. By coming together in the confederacy, the Iroquois had a strong voice when they met with the Europeans. They wanted to trade with everyone, so they decided to stay out of the European wars.

The European settlers and traders, however, still wanted the strong Iroquois warriors to help them fight. The British sent messengers to ask for their help. One chief told the governor of Canada that the Iroquois were the most important people. He said the Europeans, or the ax makers as he called them, should not tell the Iroquois what to do. "We Human Beings are the first, and we are the eldest and the greatest . . . the Human Beings [were here] before there were any Axe-Makers."

At times, the Iroquois joined sides with the people who they thought would be most helpful to them in the future. When the British began winning battles in the French and Indian War (1754–1763), the Iroquois

Onondaga and British soldiers meet around a council fire.

decided to fight alongside the British.

Then, during the American Revolutionary War (1775–1783), the Iroquois Confederacy split apart. The confederacy met in council to talk about the war. The chiefs could not agree. The Mohawk, Onondaga, Cayuga, and Seneca fought for the British. The Oneida and Tuscarora

Joseph Brant

joined the Americans. When the British lost the war, they remained in power in Canada. In return for his loyalty during the war, Mohawk Chief Joseph Brant asked the British for land in Canada. The British agreed.

31

"OUR FOREFATHERS OWNED THIS GREAT LAND"

After the Revolutionary War, the American Army punished the Iroquois for fighting with the British. The troops destroyed their villages and burned their crops. Many more Iroquois escaped to Canada. Those that

American General John Sullivan's Army destroyed 40 Iroquois villages during the Revolutionary War. After the war ended, the Army continued to burn down villages.

32

stayed in the United States watched as American farmers bought their best farmland. The remaining land became reservations for the Iroquois.

The reservations, however, were not large enough for crops or hunting. The Iroquois had to either work for the Americans or sell their land to make money. By the early 1800s, the Iroquois had sold much of their reservation land for small amounts of money. In 1805, Red Jacket, a Seneca chief, spoke of the loss of land: "There was a time when our forefathers owned this great [land] . . . from the rising to the setting sun. The Great Spirit had made it for the use of Indians."

Red Jacket

Life on the reservations was terrible. Many people did not have jobs, and they stopped practicing the traditional ceremonies. In 1799, a Seneca chief named Handsome Lake dreamed that the Creator spoke to him. Handsome Lake's New Religion or Good Message told the Iroquois to bring back the old ceremonies. Handsome Lake encouraged the men to learn how to farm so they could feed their families.

In 1830, the United States passed the Indian Removal Act. This law gave the U.S. government the power to take Indian lands in the eastern United States

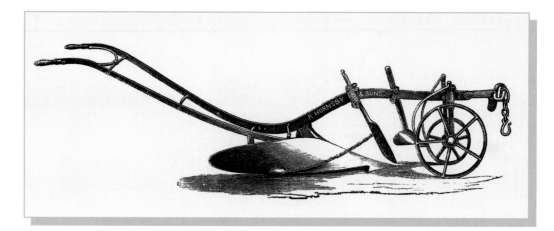

Chief Handsome Lake encouraged the Iroquois to farm with European tools, like the plow.

and make the native people move to land west of the Mississippi River. Most of the Iroquois fought in court and were able to keep their reservation land in New York. Some Cayuga and Seneca moved to Oklahoma, and some Oneida moved to Wisconsin. Though the Iroquois had lost much, leaders such as Handsome Lake and Red Jacket reminded them that they still had their traditions.

The Iroquois have kept their traditions, such as the game of lacrosse, alive.
This photo shows the Caughnawaga Mohawks, the 1869 Canadian lacrosse champions.

THE IROQUOIS TODAY

The Iroquois have survived many changes since they first met European traders 500 years ago. Many now live and work in cities all over the United States and Canada. Their children speak English, and most go to schools outside the

The Iroquois Confederacy flag features the same pattern as the Hiawatha wampum belt.

reservations. Because few Iroquois can speak the native languages, they have recorded the languages of their elders and written dictionaries. Also, some nations have started schools to teach the languages to their children, in hopes of preserving the language.

Council fires still burn at the Onondaga reservation in New York and at the Six Nations reserve in Canada. The council fires represent the traditional Iroquois government. At Grand Council meetings, chiefs still recite the great laws of the Peacemaker. They use original wampum belts to remember and tell Iroquois history. The council chiefs work together to solve problems that face the Iroquois today.

The Iroquois protect their traditions. Some believe their ceremonies, medicine masks, and dances should be shared only with other Iroquois. But they are happy to share their social dances and traditional crafts with visitors at annual festivals. Iroquois women make cornhusk dolls and dress them with traditional clothing. They sell the

Beginning with a lawsuit in 1899, the Iroquois fought for the return of wampum belts that were wrongfully sold in 1891. Some of the belts were returned in the late 1980s.

dolls, colorful beadwork, baskets, and jewelry to visitors.

Most Iroquois are no longer farmers. Many work in nearby cities. Some work at reservation casinos where visitors can gamble or play bingo. Gambling brings money into the reservations. The Oneida reservation in New York has used the money to buy more land and build a hotel and a golf course. Some Iroquois do not want gambling on the reservations.

Traditional Iroquois dancers at a festival

39

The Mohawk have been ironworkers for more than 100 years. They have built many bridges and skyscrapers. Mohawk ironworkers helped build the Golden Gate Bridge in San Francisco. They also worked on the Empire State Building, the Chrysler Building, and the World Trade Center in New York City. When the World Trade Center was destroyed by terrorists in 2001, Mohawk workers rushed there to help search for survivors.

The Iroquois are proud of their traditions. They teach their children to respect nature, give thanks, and remember the sacred ceremonies. As Oren Lyons, an Onondaga Faithkeeper, pointed out, "The [elders] said, 'As long as there's one [Iroquois] to sing and one to dance, one to speak and one to listen, life will go on.'"

*Mohawk ironworkers helped build New York City's Columbia
Presbyterian Medical Center in the 1920s.*

GLOSSARY

alliance—an agreement between nations to work together

ceremony—traditional prayer or dance used to celebrate a special occasion

clans—groups of people related by a common ancestor

confederacy—a union of nations or tribes

gamble—to play games of chance for money

reservations—large areas of land set aside for Native Americans; in Canada, reservations are called reserves

sacred—holy or deserving great respect

wampum—small beads strung together in designs to record events

DID YOU KNOW?

- Henry Wadsworth Longfellow, an American poet, wrote *The Song of Hiawatha* in 1855. In his poem, Hiawatha is not based on the Iroquois hero. The Hiawatha in Longfellow's poem is more like a legendary Ojibwe man named Manabozho.

- The Iroquois played a game featuring sticks with nets on the end and a wood ball about the size of a grapefruit. This game is the modern game of lacrosse.

- The Iroquois used snowshoes to hunt animals in the winter. Strong hunters could travel 50 miles (80 kilometers) a day wearing snowshoes.

- Mohawk men shaved all of their hair except a piece on top. This hairstyle is still called a Mohawk.

- The laws of the Iroquois Confederacy created a fair government where each member of the tribes had a say in decisions. Some historians believe Benjamin Franklin and other Founding Fathers used this as a model when writing the U.S. Constitution.

IMPORTANT DATES

Timeline

900 B.C.	Ancestors of the Iroquois living in the southern United States move into northeastern woodlands.
1570	The Peacemaker shares the Great Law of Peace; by 1600 the Iroquois Confederacy is formed.
1634	Smallpox and measles kill one-half of the Iroquois people.
1722	The Tuscarora join as the sixth member of the Iroquois Confederacy.
1775	The Iroquois Confederacy falls apart during the American Revolutionary War.
1799	Handsome Lake brings the New Religion to the Iroquois.
1830	U.S. Congress passes the Indian Removal Act to move American Indians in the eastern United States off their lands.
1988	New York State Museum returns 12 wampum belts to Onondaga in New York.
1989	National Museum of the American Indian returns 11 wampum belts to Canadian Iroquois.
1993	Oneida reservation opens a large casino near Syracuse, New York.

IMPORTANT PEOPLE

JOSEPH BRANT (1743?–1807)
Mohawk war chief who sided with the British during the American Revolutionary War; when the British lost, he asked for land in Canada, which is now the Six Nations reserve.

HIAWATHA (?–?)
Onondaga chief who helped establish peace among the Iroquois Nations in the late 1500s

HANDSOME LAKE (1735–1815)
Seneca chief who dreamed of a new religion for the Iroquois, which combined Iroquois traditions with Christianity.

OREN LYONS (1930–)
Champion lacrosse player who was elected to the Lacrosse Hall of Fame in 1992; he was chosen the Faithkeeper of the Turtle Clan of Onondagas because of his knowledge of traditions, and he speaks all over the world on protecting the environment.

RED JACKET (1750–1830)
Famous Seneca chief who spoke at every treaty council between the Iroquois and the Europeans from 1780 to 1820; he wanted the Iroquois to stay out of the fight between the Americans and the British.

WANT TO KNOW MORE?

At the Library

Bjornlund, Lydia. *The Iroquois.* San Diego: Lucent Books, 2001.

Grack, Rachel K. *The Iroquois: Longhouse Builders.* Mankato, Minn.: Blue
Earth Books, 2003.

Kallen, Stuart. *Native Americans of the Great Lakes.* San Diego: Lucent
Books, 2000.

Kalman, Bobbie. *Life in a Longhouse Village.* New York: Crabtree
Publishing, 2001.

On the Web

For more information on the *Iroquois*, use FactHound

to track down Web sites related to this book.

1. Go to *www.facthound.com*

2. Type in a search word related to this book
    or this book ID: 0756512727

3. Click on the *Fetch It* button.

Your trusty FactHound will fetch the best Web sites for you!

On the Road

Iroquois Indian Museum
324 Caverns Road
Howes Cave, NY 12092
518/296-8949
To see a collection of modern
Iroquois art, a children's museum,
and two log homes from the 1800s
in a large nature park

Woodland Cultural Centre
184 Mohawk St.
Brantford, Ontario, Canada
519/759-2650
To see more than 25,000 items,
including historic Iroquois clothing,
furniture, crafts, photographs, and a
rebuilt longhouse from the 1800s

Look for more We the People books about this era:

The Alamo

The Arapaho and Their History

The Battle of the Little Bighorn

The Buffalo Soldiers

The California Gold Rush

The Cherokee and Their History

The Chumash and Their History

The Creek and Their History

The Erie Canal

Great Women of Pioneer America

Great Women of the Old West

The Lewis and Clark Expedition

The Louisiana Purchase

The Mexican War

The Ojibwe and Their History

The Oregon Trail

The Pony Express

The Powhatan and Their History

The Pueblo and Their History

The Santa Fe Trail

The Sioux and Their History

The Trail of Tears

The Transcontinental Railroad

The Wampanoag and Their History

The War of 1812

A complete list of We the People titles is available on our Web site:
www.compasspointbooks.com

INDEX

About the Author

Genevieve St. Lawrence is a freelance author of more than 30 nonfiction books for children. A graduate of Gustavus Adolphus College in St. Peter, Minnesota, she lives and writes in Minnesota.